YOUR KNOWLEDGE HAS VALUE

- We will publish your bachelor's and master's thesis, essays and papers

- Your own eBook and book - sold worldwide in all relevant shops

- Earn money with each sale

Upload your text at www.GRIN.com and publish for free

Bibliographic information published by the German National Library:

The German National Library lists this publication in the National Bibliography; detailed bibliographic data are available on the Internet at http://dnb.dnb.de .

Imprint:

Copyright © 2009 GRIN Verlag, Open Publishing GmbH
Print and binding: Books on Demand GmbH, Norderstedt Germany
ISBN: 978-3-668-12249-9

This book at GRIN:

http://www.grin.com/en/e-book/175685/icann-the-organization-and-governance-of-the-internet

Ludwig Bäßler

ICANN. The Organization and Governance of the Internet

GRIN Publishing

GRIN - Your knowledge has value

Since its foundation in 1998, GRIN has specialized in publishing academic texts by students, college teachers and other academics as e-book and printed book. The website www.grin.com is an ideal platform for presenting term papers, final papers, scientific essays, dissertations and specialist books.

Visit us on the internet:

http://www.grin.com/

http://www.facebook.com/grincom

http://www.twitter.com/grin_com

The Organization and Governance of the Internet

Ludwig Bäßler, 2009

Contents

1 Introduction 3

2 The history of ICANN 3

3 Organization and structure 4
   3.1 Organizational bodies 4
   3.2 Accountability 6
   3.3 Decision-making process 6

4 The tasks of ICANN 7
   4.1 Domain Name System 7
   4.2 Accrediting registrars 9
   4.3 Root System 10
   4.4 Uniform Domain-Name Dispute-Resolution Policy 10
   4.5 Universal resolvability 11

5 Criticism & problems 12
   5.1 New top-level domain system 12
   5.2 Consensus model 13
   5.3 Grace period 14
   5.4 Contract with the U.S. government 14

Sources 16

1 Introduction

"When I took office, only high energy physicists had ever heard of what is called the Worldwide Web... Now even my cat has its own page."[1]
This quotation by Bill Clinton from 1996 describes exactly the evolution of the Internet. Only a few years ago, hardly no one of us had any idea what the Internet really was, what it would be good for, or how we might use it. Today most of us could not even live without it just for one day. We permanently use the Internet for so many purposes. News, entertainment, communication, file sharing, shopping, education and many more things like these. Nowadays the Internet is also a basic element for various sectors which totally depend on it, such as telecommunication, the economy or infrastructure. But how does this highly complicated system actually work? And how is it possible that each web site can be reached any time by everyone worldwide?

2 The History of ICANN

When the Internet was in its small beginnings, a group of volunteers, called the National Science Foundation (NSF), and the U.S. government contractors controlled the Domain Name System which ensures to find a certain website. In 1992, the private company Network Solutions was contracted by the NSF to manage the top-level domains (TLD) .com, .org and .net. Together with the Internet Assigned Numbers Authority (IANA) it controlled the root system (see 4.3).
When the Internet grew bigger and bigger, the assignment of domain names was not that easy anymore because popular .com names became rare and so Network Solution's private monopoly was criticized. Also the governments of some countries expressed concern over the U.S. control of the root system. As

---

[1] Bill Clinton, URL: http://www.quotationspage.com/quote/31751.html

Network Solution's contract with the NSF expired in 1997, the Department of Commerce came up with a plan, known as the White Paper, to transfer the administration of the Domain Name System to a private, non-profit corporation and thus improve its technical management. Then in 1998, a group of computer scientists, Internet service providers and trademark interests met to form an initial Board of Directors and shortly after that, on September 18, the **Internet Corporation for Assigned Names and Numbers (ICANN)** was founded as a private, non-profit corporation in Marina Del Rey, California. This is also said to be cyberspace's own *"constitutional moment"*[2].

ICANN's major objective is to manage the Domain Name System to ensure that every Internet address only exists once so users can get to the website they want. Without ICANN's coordination of these unique identifiers across the world, we would not have one global Internet.

Over the last years ICANN made important decisions. It came up with the Uniform Domain-Name Dispute-Resolution Policy (UDRP) so that trademarks cannot be abused any longer. In 2001 and 2002, seven new top-level domains (.biz, .info, .name, .pro, .aero, .coop and .museum) were introduced and followed by .eu, .travel, .jobs, .cat and .mobi in 2005 and .asia in 2006, when the contract with ICANN was renewed and a new Memorandum of Understanding was signed, too, with the United States Department of Commerce to clarify the relationship with the U.S. government.

3 Organization and Structure

3.1 Organizational bodies

"At present, ICANN is formally organized as a non-profit corporation for

---

[2] Kathleen E. Fuller, "ICANN: The debate over governing the internet", URL: http://www.law.duke.edu/journals/dltr/ARTICLES/2001dltr0002.html, p. 1.

charitable and public purposes under the California Nonprofit Public Benefit Corporation Law."[3]

ICANN has different organizational bodies. The structure is visualized in the following Figure:

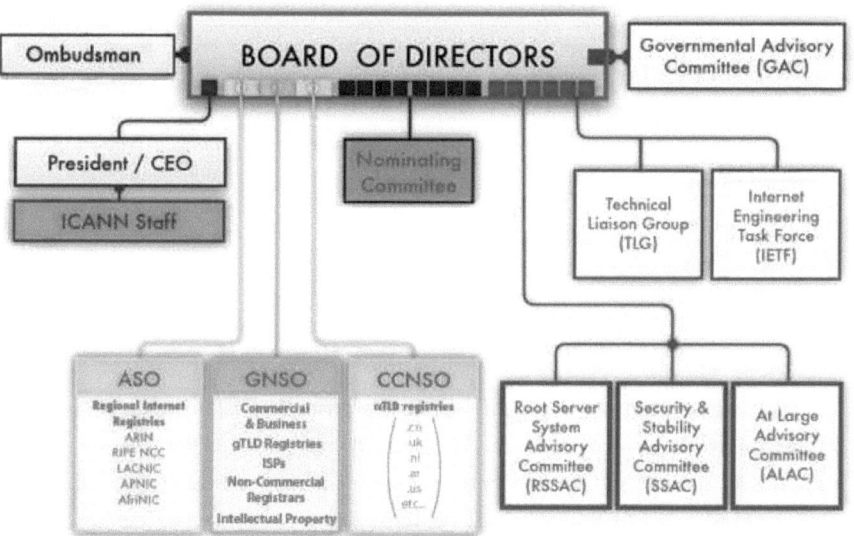

Source: http://www.icann.org/images/org-structure.jpg

The management of ICANN is done by a **Board of Directors**. Eight members are selected through an independent Nominating Committee, six by the supporting organizations, and another six by advisory committees. In addition, the advisory committees have non-voting members. Their number is variable. The President and CEO Paul Twomey is also part of the Board. He directs the work of ICANN staff, who is based all over the globe. The ICANN staff helps with coordination, management and implementing decisions made by the supporting organizations.

ICANN has three **supporting organizations** at the moment. The Generic

---

[3] Wikipedia, "ICANN", URL: http://en.wikipedia.org/wiki/Icann

Names Supporting Organization (GNSO) deals with policy making on generic top-level domains. The Country Code Names Supporting Organization (ccNSO) deals with policy making on country-code top-level domains. The Address Supporting Organization (ASO) deals with policy making on IP addresses.[4]

The **advisory committees**, which provide advice and recommendations, represent government organizations, technical and security groups, and also average Internet users in the At Large Advisory Committee (ALAC). Independent reviewing of the work of the ICANN staff and Board is carried out by an Ombudsman.

3.2 Accountability

ICANN is held accountable externally as well as internally. As ICANN is incorporated under the law of the State of California, it must follow the laws of the United States and can be taken to court in case of a violation. The directors are also responsible for upholding their duties under the corporation law because ICANN is a non-profit public benefit corporation. The internal accountabilities to the community are ICANN's bylaws, the ICANN Board, the Nominating Committee, senior staff that must be elected annually and *"three different dispute resolution procedures"[5]*. These are the Ombudsman, an Independent Review Panel and the Board reconsideration committee.

3.3 Decision-making process

Normally changes come from suggestions by one of the supporting organizations, where they are also discussed and followed by a report which is

---

[4] Ibid.
[5] "About ICANN", URL: http://losangeles2007.icann.org/icann, p. 4.

put out for public review. If any other group within ICANN's system is affected with the suggested changes, it takes a look on it, and after that the result is put out for public review one more time. Then the ICANN Board of Directors gets a report including all the previous discussions and a list of recommendations. The issue is discussed by the Board and it *"either approves the changes, approves some and rejects others, rejects all of them, or sends the issue back down to one of the supporting organizations to review, often with an explanation as to what the problems are that need to be resolved before it can be approved."*[6] Until all parts of ICANN make a compromise or the Board of Directors makes a decision on one of the reports, the process is rerun.

4 The tasks of ICANN

4.1 Domain Name System

One of the main tasks of ICANN is managing the Domain Name System, which is created for easier access to the Internet. Each Internet address disposes of two basic components, a domain name and an Internet protocol number. You can imagine the Domain Name System as a kind of electronic telephone book. In a telephone book a person's name is associated with a given phone number. In the same way, the Domain Name System associates a domain name with an Internet protocol number.

A domain name, also often just referred to as a domain, e.g. icann.org, consist of two elements. The part to the left of the dot is the **domain name** itself, sometimes also called second-level domain, which is registered and then used to provide online systems, such as websites and email. There a several registrars who are responsible for the sale of these domains. An example for this is DENIC eG for all the domains under the TLD .de. As ICANN governs all the TLDs, the terms and conditions are defined by ICANN with the cooperation

---

[6] Ibid., p. 3.

of each TLD registry.

The dot is followed by the **top-level domain** (TLD). TLDs are divided in several categories. Generic top-level domains include the ones created in the early development of the Domain Name System like .com, .net or .org. Country-code top-level domains are used by a country or a dependent territory e.g. .de for Germany, or .us for the United States. Furthermore there are sponsored top-level domains, generic-restricted top-level domains and one infrastructure top-level domain. Overall there are 291 top-level domains and ICANN already approved a system for unrestricted generic top-level domains, which is expected to be implemented in the second quarter of 2009. This means organizations or cities could apply for their own top-level domain such as .nyc for New York City.

But the main way computer addresses are specified on the network is through 32-bit numbers, the so-called Internet protocol (IP) numbers. In ICANN's case the number for their website is "192.0.34.163". As it would be pretty hard for human beings to keep such numbers in mind for every website they like to remember, the Domain Name System was invented. It links an exact series of letters with the same exact series of numbers, so the host computer can translate the domain name, which is typed in by an Internet user, into its corresponding Internet protocol number. As a consequence, messages can be sent and received.

Apart from making the Internet much easier generally, the Domain Name System has also the advantage that it is an extremely flexible system. Websites do not have to be tied to one specific computer, as the link between one domain and its Internet protocol address can be changed fast and easily. If such a change occurs, the entire Internet will recognize it within 48 hours because the Domain Name System infrastructure is updating constantly.[7] ICANN takes care of the Domain Name System. Thus it has a consistent and stable environment. In addition to it, an addressing system is provided, too, so people can find specific websites on the Internet. What is more, it is also the

---

[7] "About ICANN", URL: http://losangeles2007.icann.org/icann, p. 1.

basis for many other online uses such as emails. So it is very important that ICANN makes sure that the domain names which are used are unique, and that there are not two equal Internet protocol numbers possible at all. ICANN is also the main store for Internet protocol numbers, from which regional registries are supplied and later they are distributed to the individual network providers.

4.2 Accrediting registrars

Another objective of ICANN is accrediting the domain name registrars. *""Accredit" means to identify and set minimum standards for the performance of registration functions, to recognize persons or entities meeting those standards, and to enter into an accreditation agreement that sets forth the rules and procedures applicable to the provision of Registrar Services."*[8] So if a company wants to become a registrar, who has direct access to the top-level domains designated by ICANN, they first have to meet certain qualifications. ICANN runs various background investigations to ascertain that the entity is suitable for becoming an accredited TLD registrar. But ICANN can also revoke the accreditation. Just recently ICANN decided to de-accredit EstDomains in November 2008, after the president of this domain name registrar had been found guilty of credit card fraud, money laundering and document forgery by an Estonian court. EstDomains was among the largest registrars worldwide with over 280,000 registered domains. But it was repeatedly criticized by security experts for some time because it did not ban illegal activities. Tens of thousands of malicious sites were registered under EstDomains and used for spam, spyware or other criminal activities. EstDomains was even seen as *"a haven for cyber criminals"*[9] because it was the largest registrar for online

---

[8] ICANN FAQ, URL: http://www.icann.org/en/faq/
[9] Brian Krebs, "ICANN De-Accredits EstDomains for CEO's Fraud Convictions",
URL: http://voices.washingtonpost.com/securityfix/2008/10/icann_deaccredits_estdomains.html

criminals. But of course not all of the registered domains were bad. Other organizations, which were approved by ICANN, will now take on these legal domains.

4.3 Root System

Another ICANN activity is working with the operators of the **root servers**. *"There are 13 root servers – or, more accurately, there are 13 IP addresses on the Internet where root servers can be found"[10]*. The different physical locations of the servers that have one of the 13 addresses can vary. Each server has a copy of a file including a master list of all top-level domain names, which is refreshed on a daily basis. The registries' addresses of each top-level domain can also be found on this list. The root servers are also a very important part without which the Internet could not function. ICANN ensures they stay up-to-date with changes and advances of the Internet.

4.4 Uniform Domain-Name Dispute-Resolution Policy

The **Uniform Domain-Name Dispute-Resolution Policy (UDRP)** is a further important task. This process was established by ICANN to prevent trademarks from being abused. In this respect, "cybersquatting" became a household word. People register domain names which are equal or similar to popular trademarks or well-known persons. They hope they get more clicks on their website, or can sell it to those owning the trademark by making a great profit out of it. The UDRP is an attempt to provide a quick and cheap resolution for domain name disputes without the traditional court system.
Every domain registrant must agree to the UDRP and assure that the registered name will not infringe upon or otherwise violate the rights of any

---

[10] "About ICANN", URL: http://losangeles2007.icann.org/icann, p. 2.

third party. Third parties can file a complaint if a domain name is similar or identical to a trademark the complainant owns, the registrant does not have any legitimate interest and if he is using it in bad faith. In the UDRP process a panel will then consider whether the registrant only registered the domain name to sell it to the trademark owner, to disrupt business of competitors, or for commercial gain of his website through confusion with the complainant's trademark. If the UDRP proceeding is lost by the registrant, he must bring in a lawsuit against the trademark holder to keep ICANN from transferring the domain name. The trademark holder may also file a lawsuit if he loses.[11]

An outstanding example for this is the case *"Madonna Ciccone, p/k/a Madonna v. Dan Parisi and "Madonna.com""*[12] in 2000. Dan Parisi, a businessman from New York, registered the website www.madonna.com in 1989 and also offered pornographically content on it. Madonna did not want her reputation to be tattered and accused Parisi of using the website only with the intent of profiting from the popularity of the celebrity. Madonna argued that Parisi had no legitimate interest in the domain name and that she already registered her name as a trademark in 1979. The domain name was turned over to Madonna after the arbitration panel had decided that the registrant Dan Parisi violated against all three factors mentioned above. Other celebrities like Robert de Niro or Julia Roberts also retrieved their domain names through this arbitration procedure, whereas the singer Sting lost his case because "sting" is a common English word and not his real name.

4.5 Universal resolvability

In conclusion, ICANN is keen on being a watchful institution to oversee all the different and unique identifiers which are connected over a large worldwide

---

[11] Wikipedia, "Uniform Domain-Name Dispute-Resolution Policy",
URL: http://en.wikipedia.org/wiki/UDRP
[12] WIPO Arbitration and Mediation Center, "Madonna Ciccone, p/k/a Madonna v. Dan Parisi and "Madonna.com" Case No. D2000-0847",
URL: http://www.wipo.int/amc/en/domains/decisions/html/2000/d2000-0847.html

network. So computers can find each other on the Internet, which is often called a *"universal resolvability"[13]*. This means you get the same predictable results from any point in the world, as soon as you get access to the Internet. Otherwise the Internet would just totally depend on your individual location in the world.

5 Criticism & Problems

5.1 New top-level domain system

ICANN has to face harsh criticism for various reasons. One point is the new planned system for **unrestricted generic top-level domains**. The reasons for this new system is that ICANN wants to provide improved choices for domain name holders permitting any character string as a TLD, and also the dominance of the TLD .com. There is a total amount of 78 million registered .com domains at the moment, whereas the TLD .biz, which was created in 2001, still has only 2 million registrations, and thus has even less than e.g. .de with more than 12 million registrations.[14]

A lot of companies are already buying up different domains including their name or such which are similar to their trademark to prevent cybersquatting. So, for example google.biz, google.net or google.info all redirect you to google.com and when you type in newyorktimes.com you will be linked immediately to the main domain nytimes.com. This method speaks in favor of a good sense of business because like that it is easier for a user just guessing a domain name. However, with the possibility to choose the TLD yourself, many companies are afraid of the fact that their brand names might be hijacked. The New York Times for example would not want someone to register .nyt, .nytimes, or .newyorktimes.

---

[13] "About ICANN", URL: http://losangeles2007.icann.org/icann, p. 2.
[14] Robert Minto, "Websites: New Domain Name keeps things simple",
   URL: http://www.ft.com/cms/s/0/281dc8c0-bf51-11dd-ae63-0000779fd18c.html

ICANN promises that only certain companies and individuals will have the right to register an own TLD, and with an estimated price of $185,000 and a $75,000 fee a year it will be hardly possible for an unauthorized person to register such a domain. However, with ICANN's original intent not to control the content of the Internet, this is seen critically, too.

Another problem is that blacklisting could also be negatively affected. The objective of blacklisting is to identify and ban illegal websites. It already takes some time for blacklists to find and classify the approximately new 3,500 websites coming online every day. With the new open system it will become even harder.

Hence it is very important that ICANN really keeps up with the planned measures and it will not be too easy to register any domain name you want.

5.2 Consensus model

The way ICANN governs the Domain Name System is criticized, too. Outside its relationship with the government the **consensus model** gives ICANN's action certain legitimacy. *"As a private-public partnership, ICANN is dedicated… to achieving broad representation of global Internet communities; and to developing policy appropriate to its mission through bottom-up, consensus-based processes"*[15]. So if this model is followed by ICANN, it is only a consolidation to express the will of the Internet community. But critics argue that this model is wrong for Internet governance. For example when it comes to issues like who is able to become a domain name registrar or a resolution between competing domain name registrations this could not be solved by this way because *"these questions involve competing claims of right, and are thus not particularly well-suited to resolution by consensus."*[16]

On the other hand ICANN is criticized that it does not really act by consensus

---

[15] "ICANN Factsheet", URL: http://www.icann.org/en/factsheets/factsheet.html
[16] Fuller, p. 4.

e.g. the initial board of directors was chosen clandestinely although ICANN's structure should be open to the public. Decisions ought to be the outcome of a rich, searching conversation with all persons involved. Another example is that ICANN decided to retain some board members past the expiration. So it is questionable if the governance is really done by consensus or the commitment to openness and representativeness is just a sham.

5.3 Grace period

When somebody registers a domain name under a generic top-level domain, ICANN grants the new user a **grace period**. That means that for a period five days the registrant can, in case he changes his mind, undo the registration free of charge. Now there are people who register a domain name for the grace period, and if they do not have the wanted commercial success, they delete it and try out other domain names. This is called "domain tasting" and causes unessential traffic to the Domain Name System and is also seen to be unfair to ingenious users.

There is also the process of "domain kiting", where the registrant deletes his domain name before the five-day grace period, then re-registers it immediately and repeats this procedure as long as he wants. So he owns a domain name without actually paying for it.

Therefore it is demanded that every registrant needs to pay if he registers a domain name as it is the case with most of the country code top-level domains, or at least that there is more precise observation.

5.4 Contract with the U.S. government

One of the major critical points is that the control of the Internet's core address system lies in the hands of the **USA** because ICANN is mandated by the US department of commerce. There are a huge number of states represented in the Governmental Advisory Committee, but they can only give recommendations and so the USA has the power.

An example is the introduction of .xxx as a top-level domain for all websites with pornographic content. This was rejected by ICANN after enormous pressure was put on the Bush-government with several religious anti-xxx-campaigns. Theoretically the department of commerce could also turn off all .ir websites for the Iran, and thus potential enemies could be plunged into chaos.

A lot of countries like China, Saudi Arabia or the Iran want the Internet governance to be *"truly international, with ICANN either dismantled or altered to include formal representation for each country."*[17] So far domains name can only be in Roman characters and not in languages like Chinese or Arabic. But the demands for a multilingual Internet are big. Although ICANN is already testing domain names in non roman characters and planning to implement them someday, China e.g. has already threatened to make their own Internet network and tested domain names in Chinese which are not compatible with our existing Internet. A suggestion is also to give the control over the Domain Name System to the International Telecommunications Union, an organization connected to the United Nations, which is already running the telephone numbering system.

To avoid this criticism ICANN created the Internet Governance Forum, which was already seen, by some, as the slowly beginning of an abolition of the U.S. control via ICANN. But under closer scrutiny it is only a forum for discussions and cannot make decisions.

In 2005 the contract between the US department of commerce and ICANN was renewed for at least five years, so serious objections of some critics about a new and more international control of the Internet will not come to an end.

---

[17] Kate Mackenzie, "FT Briefing: Internet governance",
URL: http://www.ft.com/cms/s/2/e50be7f4-56b4-11da-b98c-00000e25118c.html,
p. 2.

Sources

Cockrill, Howie. "Tech News: ICANN & Domain Names" 17 Aug, 2007. URL: http://beatblog.typepad.com/melon/2007/08/tech-news-icann.html [19 Jan, 2009]

Fältström, Patrik. "What is Good Policy for a Domain Name Registry?" 9 Jan, 2009. URL: http://www.circleid.com/posts/20090109_good_policy_domain_ name_registry/ [20 Jan, 2009]

Froomkin, A. Michael. "WRONG TURN IN CYBERSPACE: USING ICANN TO ROUTE AROUND THE APA AND THE CONSTITUTION" 1 Oct, 2000. URL: http://personal.law.miami.edu/~froomkin/articles/icann.pdf [24 Oct, 2008]

Fuller, Kathleen E. "ICANN: The debate over governing the internet" 14 Feb,2001. URL: http://www.law.duke.edu/journals/dltr/ARTICLES/2001dltr0002.html [11 Sept, 2008]

Hofmann, Jeanette. "Internet Corporation for Assigned Names and Numbers" 2007. URL: http://www.globaliswatch.org/files/pdf/GISW_ICANN.pdf [7 Dec, 2008]

Hruska, Joel. "ICANN plan for new TLDS comes under barrage of criticism" 16 Dec, 2008. URL: http://arstechnica.com/news.ars/post/20081216-icannplan- for-new-tlds-comes-under-barrage-of-criticism.html [23 Jan, 2009]

ICANN, Official Site. URL: http://icann.org/
Internet Governance Project. "What to Do About ICANN: A Proposal for

Structural Reform" 5 Apr, 2005.
URL: http://www.internetgovernance.org/pdf/igp-icannreform.pdf [6 Nov, 2008]

Krebs, Brian. "ICANN De-Accredits EstDomains for CEO's Fraud Convictions"
29 Oct, 2008.
URL: http://voices.washingtonpost.com/securityfix/2008/10/icann_deaccredits_
estdomains.html [22 Jan, 2009]

Los Angeles 2007. "About ICANN". URL: http://losangeles2007.icann.org/icann
[6 Nov, 2008]

Mackenzie, Kate. "FT Briefing: Internet governance" 16 Nov, 2005. URL:
http://www.ft.com/cms/s/2/e50be7f4-56b4-11da-b98c-00000e25118c.html
[6 Nov, 2008]

Mackenzie, Kate. "Internet governance remains in US hands" 16 Nov, 2005.
URL: http://www.ft.com/cms/s/2/d5c71646-56a1-11da-b98c-
00000e25118c.html [6 Nov, 2008]

Macnair, Ed. "Blacklists will be swamped by domain name explosion"
22 Sep, 2008. URL: http://www.ft.com/cms/s/0/2f172f76-84a1-11dd-b148-
0000779fd18c.html [5 Nov, 2008]

Maher, David. "What's going on at ICANN in Cairo" 6 Nov, 2008. URL:
http://www.circleid.com/posts/20081106_whats_going_on_icann_in_cairo/
[7 Nov, 2008]

Mikko. "Case EstDomains".
URL: http://www.f-secure.com/weblog/archives/00001522.html [22 Jan, 2009]

Minto, Robert. "Websites: New domain name keeps things simple"
2 Dec, 2008. URL: http://www.ft.com/cms/s/0/281dc8c0-bf51-11dd-ae63-
0000779fd18c.html [25 Dec, 2008]

Mueller, Milton. "ICANN and Internet governance sorting through debris of
selfregulation"
6 Dec, 1999. URL: http://www.icannwatch.org/archive/muell.pdf
[25 Nov, 2008]

Oden, Matthias. "Domainvergabe: Nach .com jetzt .alleistmöglich"
26 Jun, 2008. URL: http://www.ftd.de/technik/medien_internet/:Domainvergabe
%20Nach/378303.html [24 Oct, 2008]

Post, David G. "Cyberspace's Constitutional Moment" Nov, 1998. URL:
http://www.temple.edu/lawschool/dpost/DNSGovernance.htm [14 Dec, 2008]

Rosenbach, Marcel. "Die Machtfrage" Mar, 2007. URL:
http://wissen.spiegel.de/wissen/image/show.html?did=52058391&aref=image0
36/2007/06/26/ROSPC200700300840086.PDF&thumb=false [24 Oct, 2008]

Spiegel Online. "Madonna.com: Das „Material Girl" bekommt seine Web-
Adresse" 17 Oct, 2000.
URL: http://www.spiegel.de/netzwelt/web/0,1518,98388,00.html [18 Jan, 2009]

Steel, Emily. "New Domain Names Put Name Brands in a Bind" 5 Nov, 2008.
URL: http://online.wsj.com/article/SB122583938093998683.html?mod=
googlenews_wsj [6 Nov, 2008]

Tiede, Jennifer. "Frage des Tages: Welchen Einfluss hat ICANN?"
16 Nov, 2005. URL: http://www.ftd.de/technik/it_telekommunikation/30789.html
[5 Nov, 2008]

Uhe, Bianca. "ICANN". URL: http://ig.cs.tuberlin.
de/oldstatic/w2000/ir1/referate2/k-4a/bianca.html [24 Oct, 2008]

Waters, Richards. "US keeps control of web address" 30 Sep, 2006. URL:
http://www.ft.com/cms/s/0/ba69e2f2-501f-11db-9d85-0000779e2340.html
[15 Nov, 2008]

Weinberg, Jonathan. "ICANN AND THE PROBLEM OF LEGITIMACY" 2000.
URL: http://www.law.wayne.edu/weinberg/legitimacy.pdf [6 Dec, 2008]

Wikipedia. "ICANN". URL: http://en.wikipedia.org/wiki/Icann [6 Nov, 2008]

Wikipedia, "Uniform Domain-Name Dispute-Resolution Policy", URL:
http://en.wikipedia.org/wiki/UDRP [15 Nov, 2008]

Wikipedia. "Top-Level Domain". URL: http://en.wikipedia.org/wiki/Toplevel_
domain [8 Jan, 2009]

Williams, Frances. "UN agency warns on cybersquatting" 27 Mar, 2008. URL:
http://www.ft.com/cms/s/0/33040a58-fc1d-11dc-9229-000077b07658.html
[10 Nov, 2008]

YOUR KNOWLEDGE HAS VALUE